FOR SALE BY OWNER

A No-Nonsense Guide to Getting the Best Price for Your House

PROBUS PUBLISHING COMPANY
Chicago, Illinois

© 1990, Ceil Lohmar

ALL RIGHTS RESERVED. No part of this publication may be reproduced, stored in a retrieval system, or transmitted by any means, electronic, mechanical, photocopying, recording or otherwise, without the prior written permission of the publisher and the copyright holder.

This publication is designed to provide accurate and authoritative information in regard to the subject matter covered. It is sold with the understanding that the publisher is not engaged in rendering legal, accounting or other professional service.

Library of Congress Cataloging-in-Publication Data

Lohmar, Ceil.
    For sale by owner : a no-nonsense guide to getting the best price for your house / Ceil Lohmar.
        p.   cm.
    Includes index.
    ISBN 1-55738-161-5 : $9.95
    1. House selling. 2. Real estate business. I. Title
HD1379.L647 1990
333.33'83—dc20   90-47655
                                                                                                       CIP

Printed in the United States of America

BP

1   2   3   4   5   6   7   8   9   0

CONTENTS

What This Book Is All About   **vii**

STEP 1: Getting Ready to Sell   **1**
    Make your decorating scheme clean
      and uncluttered   2
    Exit your personality   3
    Divide up the tasks of preparing and
      showing your home   6
    Explore the market where you're likely
      to buy   9

**STEP 2: Picking Your Team, Planning
      Your Game**   **11**
    Choose a mortgage lender to
      qualify buyers   12
    Choose a legal expert to hold the
      earnest money and document the sale   16
    Plan your sale promotion by
      studying your competition   18
    Strengthen your promotions with forms—
      Visitor Sign-In Sheet, Information
      on Home For Sale Sheet
      and Offer Worksheet   20

STEP 3: Creating Your Mini Market at the Open House — 27
- Reap the open house benefits — 28
- Overcome the negative, accentuate the positive — 30
- Aim for people, people, people — 32
- Wear not emotions on thy sleeve — 35
- Allow time for your home to speak on its own behalf — 35

STEP 4: Reaching People — 37
- Make sure your neighbors are the first to know — 38
- Pound a "For Sale" sign in your front yard — 40
- Write simple ads — 42
- Refuse agents' one-buyer listings—at first — 44
- Expand your word-of-mouth team — 45

STEP 5: Fetching a Price — 49
- Ask a "good" price — 50
- Know what you can buy for the money — 52
- Weigh your asking price against financing — 53
- Listen to buyers — 54
- Free yourself from myths — 55
- Honor thy first offer — 56

STEP 6: Negotiating an Offer — 59
- Toughen up for shockingly low offers — 61
- Limit negotiations to the information on the Offer Worksheet — 62
- Refuse to lower the price for an offer with contingencies — 64
- Contact your teammate—the mortgage loan officer — 66
- Weigh, again, financing with price — 66
- Use time to your advantage — 70

STEP 7: Closing the Deal   **75**
    Anticipate that you'll be needed   76
    Contact your teammate—the legal expert   77
    Keep on top of the sale   79
    Stick—like glue—to your closing date   81
    Congratulate yourself   82

Appendix: Choosing a Real Estate Agent   **83**

Index and Glossary   **87**

WHAT THIS BOOK IS ALL ABOUT

"Is this a good time to sell?" If you're thinking about selling your home, you've probably already asked yourself that question many times.

I had frequently heard that question asked during the years when I was selling real estate. And, I hear it now when I'm teaching seminars to owners selling their homes themselves.

Obviously, you can't do anything about the current economic times; fortunately, you can do plenty about the selling. *For Sale By Owner: A No-Nonsense Guide to Getting the Best Price for Your House* presents you with a "new school" of home-selling ideas. Its goal is to enable you to sell your home more successfully, whatever the times.

It's the "Sale" in *For Sale By Owner* that this book is all about. It's not about how to be an expert on mortgage financing nor is it about how to complete your own legal documents. I suggest that you leave those details to the experts—at zero or nominal cost to you.

Having experts "on call" will enable you to concentrate your time and effort where it counts: *Making your home buyable and finding buyers.*

The most important trait, whatever the reason behind your selling, is a strong desire to do it yourself.

Then what? The following are personality traits I've observed in people who have been successful:

- A willingness to spend time and energy saving money.
- A creative mind open to different ideas.
- A streak of independence.
- A curiosity about the subject.
- An eagerness to discover more.

If you fit this profile, the rest is easy. Follow me.

Ceil Lohmar

STEP 1

GETTING READY TO SELL

When you open the door to the first buyer, you should already be prepared to close the deal. Have the track cleared from start to finish. The hard work you do *now* in getting ready to sell will make it easy for a buyer to buy.

To get ready you'll need to:

- MAKE YOUR DECORATING SCHEME CLEAN AND UN-CLUTTERED
- EXIT YOUR PERSONALITY
- DIVIDE UP THE TASKS OF PREPARING AND SHOWING YOUR HOME
- EXPLORE THE MARKET WHERE YOU'RE LIKELY TO BUY

Picture handing over the title of your home to a buyer who is giving you money. Hold that picture as your goal until the deal is done. Boast, like business professional Lee Iacocca, "If you can buy a better home, buy it."

Show your home to its very best advantage. Oversee everything and don't neglect details. Be judgmental, critical, evaluative of the work you and everyone else does to prepare and display your property. Then ask yourself, can anything still be improved? Run the show. Be the boss.

MAKE YOUR DECORATING SCHEME CLEAN AND UNCLUTTERED

Then maintain that clean, uncluttered look until your place is sold.

Furnished houses sell better than empty ones. But *clean* homes—inside and outside—sell the best. Open curtains, wash windows, shine floors, polish furniture, scour bathrooms, and scrub kitchens. Walk through the home with a bottle of spray cleaner and sponge in hand, wiping away fingerprints and smudges. Line up the items stored in cupboards and closets, ready for parade dress inspection.

Brighten light fixtures and lamps. Replace worn-out bulbs with the highest wattage bulbs that the fixtures can handle. Prepare to turn on all lights for open houses unless the room is already filled with blinding sunlight.

Reach for all the air and light you can pack into each room. When a room is dark, it sends out messages of caution and urges visitors to watch out for something hiding; that's scary. For a stranger standing at the entrance it is like looking into a dark cave.

But on the other hand, a light and sunny room sends an invitation to someone standing in the doorway: Relax, leave your cares behind and come stay for a while.

Bring the clean and uncluttered campaign into the garage, attic, basement, cellar, and carport. Take junk to the dump, have a garage sale, and call the kids. Tell them this is their last call—come get what you want now or it'll be gone. Phone the Salvation Army or the Goodwill or the second-hand store to have them stop by for what they can use. If necessary, rent a mini-storage space to hide away whatever detracts from making your home look its very best.

Critically inspect the outside. Extend the clean and uncluttered look to the landscaping, lawn, bushes, ground cover, trees, flower beds, garden, fences, and walls. Sweep the driveway, deck, patio, sidewalk, walkway, and the street curb.

I once sold a home to a couple relocating to a new city. Before the wife arrived, I met the husband several times, always after he finished work. He wanted to look at the outside of homes for sale at that particular time of day. He most looked forward to enjoying his home when he returned from work, he explained.

He only viewed the outside of homes and made a list of those he liked. When his wife arrived, she looked at the inside of the homes on his list. She chose the one she liked best. They bought it.

YOU NEVER GET A SECOND CHANCE TO MAKE A GOOD FIRST IMPRESSION!

EXIT YOUR PERSONALITY

Leave empty spaces for the buyers to envision themselves moving into your home. Wide open spaces are good for selling dreams. The less clutter, the easier it is for the buyer to look around, inspect the home, and imagine living there.

Pack away all but your choicest family pictures and vacation mementos. This exercise is good for you and for the buyers. For you, it can strengthen your goals, set you on the path of moving out, and beef up your enthusiasm for the task of selling.

For the buyers, it opens the way, in a sense, to allow them to try on the home for themselves. How would the family fit here? How would grandmother's heirloom dresser fit? And our lives, would they fit in this place?

I once showed a home to a buyer who when she saw the outside of the home said, "This is it. It's just what I've been looking for."

After seeing the inside, she slid into the front seat of my car and said, "I tried. I really wanted that home. But I couldn't put myself into living there."

I understood why. The home was a family museum packed full of the seller's family life. I bet that in 20 years nothing had been thrown out or stored away. Their past life was chronicled in faded pictures and amassed collections displayed like an exhibit at the historical society.

Q. Should we paint and re-carpet?

A. Paint only if you're too ashamed for someone to see how awful a room looks. Then take a tip from the pros who buy and resell homes all the time; paint using only off-white (not hospital white) for any room you do. A soft white color lightens the room, makes it look more open, and is least likely to be a color that a buyer dislikes. For carpeting, no matter how worn it is, I say clean it and leave it. If it needs redoing, say to the buyer, "We know a new owner will want to re-carpet so we are prepared to mark down the price by $3,000."

Q. Why not just reduce the price and say that the lowered price takes into account the need for new carpeting?

A. It's a case of turning a bad thing—worn carpeting—into a good thing: "We'll pay for the carpeting and you can pick it out yourself." The words "mark down" are magic words.

Q. Why not paint and re-carpet?

A. I have two reasons. First, a lot of buyers are like me. They like to see that a home needs redecorating. Then, if they buy, they won't feel extravagant in doing it their way. Of course, a buyer could decorate even after the sellers have just had it done. But that's wasteful. It's better to leave it for the buyers to redo. Second, if you start putting new paint on the walls and new carpet on the floor, it could stand out from the rest of the home. It not only breaks up the oneness and the all-togetherness of a home mostly decorated in 1975, but it looks suspicious. Buyers wonder, "What are they covering up?"

Q. What about valuables? We have our wedding picture in a sterling silver frame. I'd hate to have someone walk out of the house with that under his/her coat.

A. Pack it away. You won't have to worry about protecting it or packing it later. It's ready for the moving van.

Watching every move of prospective buyers and acting like a bank guard can sure take the fun out of selling. Put your mind at ease by removing temptations.

Look around. Pack away whatever might stick to sticky fingers and whatever is fragile. Clear away curiosities that investigating children and clumsy adults might destroy.

DIVIDE UP THE TASKS OF PREPARING AND SHOWING YOUR HOME

Until the home is sold, for the duration, your household should go on "Buyer Alert." The promotion technique I suggest in Step 3 is designed to funnel all lookers into scheduled open houses. But before you show your home for the first time, you must plan out how everyone in the household will cooperate in order to present your home in its best condition and, thus, make a good impression on strangers.

Make a list assigning such chores as:

- Who will make the beds?
- Who will transform the kitchen so it looks like no one eats there?
- Who will be in charge of bathroom neatness?
- Who will collect trash and take it out?
- Who will keep the outdoors picked up?
- Who will be the host or hostess at the open house?
- Who will be the assistant?
- Who will go over the following checklist before each open house?

INDOORS

- ✔ All lights on; window curtains and shades open.
- ✔ Floors clear of newspapers, shoes—anything that can be picked up and put away.
- ✔ Check floors; give them a quick sweep or vacuum them.
- ✔ Countertop and tables should be clear except for a vase of flowers.
- ✔ Toys stored away.
- ✔ Beds made hospital tight.
- ✔ Bathrooms clean as a whistle.
- ✔ Fire in the fireplace (unless it's 90° outside).
- ✔ Soft, very soft, music playing.
- ✔ Kids who get rambunctious should be given lots to keep them occupied or be farmed out.
- ✔ Pets, ditto.

OUTDOORS

- ✔ Sweep steps. People look down when they walk upstairs. Clean steps give a good first impression.

- ✔ If there is a window or mirror in the entry, make sure it sparkles.

- ✔ Turn on outside lights (unless it's noon on a sunny day).

- ✔ If you live in a condo or townhouse, make sure that finding your place is easy for a total stranger.

Decide how the telephone will be answered. There should be someone ready to pick up the phone whenever it rings. It could be *the* buyer. Playing hard to get might be good for making a date to the prom, but it isn't good for making a date for a prospective buyer to see your home. If your daily schedule leaves the telephone unattended, buy or borrow an answering machine.

Caution children in your household about leading informal tours. Only designated adults should show the home to anyone—even to friends and neighbors—with no exceptions. Instruct children that no one enters the home without an adult present and in charge, and review how they should take messages from visitors or phone callers.

EXPLORE THE MARKET WHERE YOU'RE LIKELY TO BUY

Be specific. If you can, narrow down your purchasing choice to one home. *But don't buy it.* Owning two homes is for the rich and famous. Wait to buy a home until your present sale is behind you—you'll be wiser then. Just pretend you are buying a home now. What price would you offer?

Experience being a buyer. Before you open your door to the first buyer, go feel what it's like to be a buyer. Go home shopping. Walk in buyers' shoes for know-thy-enemy preparedness.

Get a feel for price as a buyer. In each home you visit, note the sellers' asking price. Then ask yourself, "What would I pay for this?" In Step 5 I go more into pricing. For now, make a note of the sellers' price and the price you would pay.

Is the price you would offer truly realistic? Here is an exercise in realism. Take out your checkbook and pretend to write a check for $5,000 in earnest money. Would that check bounce? Where would money come from to cover the check? Would you have to sell your home first? Sell stocks or bonds? Withdraw from savings? Borrow the funds?

Rethink the price. Would you still offer the same price? Sometimes when it's your own money at stake, you tend to squeeze the price a little tighter.

> **Q.** Is there a difference in what a serious buyer will pay and the opinion of a seller as to what the price should be?
>
> **A.** Yes. Everyone—not just sellers but also the butcher, the baker, and the candlestick maker—freely expresses strong opinions on

what a price should be. The serious buyer cuts through others' opinions and gets down to the nitty-gritty of what he or she is willing to pay.

Compare look-alike homes as well as homes that offer like benefits but are otherwise different. For example: I sold a condo to a couple relocating in my area. Their top consideration was that they have the benefit of living within walking distance of downtown. They would consider nothing from any area the husband designated as, "Out where elephants go to die."

Before they settled on a condo, they looked at single-family homes, town houses, duplexes, and a fourplex apartment building. Each housing situation provided what they were looking for—a home within walking distance to downtown. How does your price compare to other types of homes with similar qualifications?

It's worthwhile to explore the competition. Make a record of the asking price. Should your price be above or below that amount? Watch how the selling goes. Check up on the price for which it sold and the time it took to sell.

STEP 2

PICKING YOUR TEAM, PLANNING YOUR GAME

Do what the young Chinese diver Tan Liangde—who almost beat Greg Louganis at the 1988 Olympics—did in Korea. Surround yourself with a supportive team and study your competition.

In Step 2 I'll show you how to prepare to be the strongest, fittest, and most competitive in your home-selling event. You'll learn to:

- CHOOSE A MORTGAGE LENDER TO QUALIFY BUYERS
- CHOOSE A LEGAL EXPERT TO HOLD THE EARNEST MONEY AND DOCUMENT THE SALE
- PLAN YOUR SALE PROMOTION BY STUDYING YOUR COMPETITION
- STRENGTHEN YOUR PROMOTING WITH FORMS—VISITOR SIGN-IN SHEET, INFORMATION ON HOME FOR SALE SHEET, AND OFFER WORKSHEET

A legal expert and a mortgage loan officer "on call" give a professional respectability to the sale of your home. A home is too expensive, too big of a debt obligation, and too legally complicated to be strictly a do-it-yourself project.

You will do best concentrating on attracting buyers and negotiating a price. After you've done this, bring in the mortgage and legal experts to finalize the sale.

Buyers will be more comfortable knowing they are not dealing exclusively with a one-time owner who may move out of town, but also with experienced businesspeople with good reputations in the community.

CHOOSE A MORTGAGE LENDER TO QUALIFY BUYERS

In the Yellow Pages under "Mortgages" or "Real Estate Loans" you'll find mortgage lenders. Call around and choose a loan officer who is helpful in answering your questions. Explain that you are selling your home yourself. Offer to distribute his or her business cards and mortgage literature at your open houses. In return, inform the loan officer that you would like him or her to qualify potential buyers for a mortgage.

> **Q.** Will giving mortgage literature be helpful in getting my home sold?
>
> **A.** Yes. Any and all information you give helps. *Information* is your salesperson.
>
> **Q.** Will mortgage loan officers give this service if they don't know me?
>
> **A.** Yes. They'll usually be happy to do so. In return, you are giving them the opportunity to reach new mortgage customers.

If you haven't been following the mortgage business in the last eight years or so, you have a lot of catching up to do. Mostly, you will find that mortgages are more expensive. And there are many choices, such as a fixed rate of interest or an adjustable rate. And points—the payment of interest in advance—are commonly charged now; they're not the exception that they were previously.

Check your existing mortgage. Telephone the holder of your mortgage. Identify yourself by your mortgage loan number and ask the following questions:

(Look up unfamiliar words in the Index and Glossary in the back of this book.)

- What is the balance owed on my mortgage?
- Is the mortgage assumable by a new owner?
- If the mortgage is assumable, under what conditions? What costs?
- Will the lender refinance the loan?
- If the lender will refinance, under what conditions and at what interest rate?
- Would the lender be interested in creating a new mortgage for a new owner? If the answer is yes, ask that the mortgage loan officer be "on call" to qualify possible buyers for an assumption, a refinance, or a new mortgage.

Get a handle on the current market. Lest you forget, mortgage lending is a fiercely competitive business. Don't let the demeanor of people in three-piece suits throw you off guard. Intimidation is the weapon of some lenders. Don't let it dull your competitive edge by keeping you uninformed as to the current mortgage market. The mortgage market is interlaced with your home market. Go ahead, ask every question you can think of including dumb questions. Your price depends

Step 2

on it. Answers to dumb questions may mean more money for you.

Know the current costs of a new mortgage. Stay on top of changes. Some lenders have a hot line that you can call for a recorded update on mortgage costs; some have a mailing list and will add your name. Most newspapers list current mortgage rates of local lenders at least once a week.

Buyers may have plans for where they will obtain a new mortgage. However, have the telephone number of your hand-picked mortgage lender available for buyers.

Q. The bank where we presently have our mortgage will offer a new mortgage to a new buyer at what seems to be a better-than-going rate. Should I get the details on that to pass along to buyers in case anyone is interested?

A. Yes, that would be a plus in selling your home. Better yet, get the *name* of a loan officer from that company. Write his/her name on the Information on Home for Sale sheet (see page 24). Offering a way to finance the home—especially when the interest rate or cost of assumption is low—makes your home more attractive to buyers.

Q. There are several ways our home could be financed. Should we suggest all the alternatives?

A. No. Offer just the name of a loan officer and his/her phone number.

Q. Why should we suggest just *one* mortgage loan officer?

A. When you offer one name you offer quick, available information; you put the financing decision in place until the buyer commits to a decision to buy the home. I've seen buyers turned off by the mumbo jumbo of creative ways of financing sellers and agents suggest. Suggesting more than one expert adviser is simply confusing.

I knew a man who had a very short career selling real estate. He was great at mortgages; lousy at getting the home sold. Buyers' eyes would glaze over as he droned on about long-term, short-term interest rates and points, on and on. He put buyers to sleep. They would go limp, losing their gung ho spirit for buying their dream house.

Consider buying down the interest rate. This is something builders of new homes often do to attract buyers. You can do it, too. Depending upon mortgage rates in your area, you may attract buyers by offering a mortgage at a lower interest rate. You, the seller, can pay to lower the interest rate. Ask your loan officer to advise you as to what advantages a buy-down mortgage would give you.

Consider offering an FHA or VA mortgage. Offering an FHA or VA mortgage can be a great advantage in selling. But, before you offer to sell to a buyer using one of these mortgages, you should be aware of additional costs you may have to pay. You may have to pay for the financing and for necessary repairs to your home.

Bring up the responsibility with your loan officer. Adjust your asking price if necessary to reimburse you for the added costs.

Consider a seller mortgage. If your present mortgage is fully paid, you can act as a lender yourself. It's worth considering. Or, if the new owners can assume your old mortgage, but they need to borrow more money, you might carry a second mortgage.

Must you get all your equity out in cash? If not, taking back a note for some of the buyers' payment may suit your investment portfolio.

Offering to be a lender to the buyers may make your property easier to sell; often for a higher price. *I am not talking about accepting no down payment, or even a low down payment.* If you even think "nothing down" forget it. If you take a mortgage, make sure the buyers make a healthy down payment, an amount of money that ensures the buyers have an investment in the property. Set it high enough so that they would hate to lose it by not keeping up the payments. And make sure a lawyer walks you through lending possibilities with the choice of mortgage instruments and safeguards necessary to be sure you get your money.

Historically, investment in mortgages has been a favorite of retired people. Farmers sell their farms to their children and live in town off the mortgage payments. Pension funds squirrel away money in home mortgages for future needs. If you lend money to buyers so they can buy your home, it can be in the form of either a first or a second mortgage. The terms can be whatever the buyers and sellers agree to and the law allows. The terms may vary. What doesn't vary is the warning: Have a lawyer representing you to write the loan documents.

CHOOSE A LEGAL EXPERT TO HOLD THE EARNEST MONEY AND DOCUMENT THE SALE

To find out who is a legal expert where you live, ask your mortgage loan officer. Customs vary in different states. You'll need someone ready to hold in trust the buyers' deposit while they arrange financing, prepare necessary legal documents, and supervise the settlement of the sale. This legal expert could be a lawyer, an escrow or title agent, or someone simply called a closer.

Recently I telephoned a loan officer in a strange town for the name of someone to document a real estate sale. The loan officer, who didn't know me, not only gave me the name of her favorite escrow agent, she said, ". . . tell her I sent you and she'll hold your hand . . ."

Hand holding is a much admired quality in someone doing legal work on a home sale. It's true with an agent involved or not. The legal expert needs the patience of a saint and the wisdom of King Solomon.

Are there impediments to a smooth sale? If so, now is the time to clear the track. Impediments could be matters such as liens, delinquent taxes, an unrecorded death, divorce proceedings or settlements. What does your state say about rights of spouses?

> **Q.** Why should we prepare to sell before we begin to promote the home? We won't need the documents prepared until after we have a buyer. That might be months away.

A. Yes, it may be months away; on the other hand, it might only take a few days to find a serious buyer. You don't want to be the one to slow down or stop a sale by not being ready.

What names appear on your proof of title? Make sure everyone who has to sign a sales contract is in agreement with you selling the property. Talk it over and reach a meeting of the minds. Selling something without the full legal right can give you a very bad headache and land you behind bars.
If other persons must be party to the sale, where will these persons be when you get an offer? Are they far away? If so, arrange ahead of time in what manner they will give their approval. The law dictates what must happen here. What forms of approval are legal in your state? A telegram, a power of attorney, a Federal Express delivery of the documents for actual signatures?

Have the telephone number of your legal expert to call when you get an offer. Generally, a buyer will have a sales contract written, but don't wait for that. Have your expert ready to write a sales contract for you, hold the earnest money check, and supervise the transfer of ownership. (See more details about this in Step 7.)

PLAN YOUR SALE PROMOTION BY STUDYING YOUR COMPETITION

Look over what's for sale out there. Decide what it's going to take to beat the competition.
What's for sale down the street, in the same condo building, or in the neighborhood? Ask yourself, "What will it take for a buyer to prefer my home?"
What is it that draws you to one home, and what is it that turns you away from another home? What is

it about some homes that you will rearrange your schedule to see, while other homes you will never have time to see? Figure out what qualities will make your home the choice one that buyers would rearrange their schedules to see.

When you look at the For Sale classified ads in the newspaper or the For Sale signs in your community, is there wording or lettering that catches your eye? Make a note to copy appealing phrases or designs.

Q. What can we learn from evaluating the promotion of other homes?

A. Check how they measure up in the following ways:

- The way you learned there would be an open house.
- The ease in touring the inside of the home.
- The factual information given you when you left.
- The sufficiency of information that would allow you to come to a decision about buying the home.
- The information you wish you had, but the seller overlooked. Resolve to provide to your prospective buyers what the competition lacks.

Resist copying real estate company tease ads. Observe how real estate companies focus their ads to attract buyers while giving little information about the home. In effect they are only hoping you'll call the agent to find out more about the home, and thus, become a client of that agent. I've seen ads with three telephone numbers to reach the agent and no address to identify the home.

You don't want to keep secret the identity of your home. Always give your address and phone number.

Q. Why should our ads be different from the real estate agents' ads?

A. You only want a buyer for *your* home. Your ads are intended to entice buyers into your home who may offer to buy it. Agents want to attract a buyer as a client; make a connection so that buyers will buy homes through them. Remember, the agent is looking for a fee for selling a home, any home. It could be the home advertised or any one of the homes listed in the multiple listing catalog.

I'll get to more on advertising in Step 4. While you are in the buyers' shoes and following ads, keep in mind how refreshingly different your ads can be with straightforward *facts* such as open house hours, the asking price and your address and phone numbers.

STRENGTHEN YOUR PROMOTIONS WITH FORMS—VISITOR SIGN-IN SHEET, INFORMATION ON HOME FOR SALE AND OFFER WORKSHEET

Have a pen with the Visitor Sign-In Sheet. Prepare to ask visitors to sign in by giving their names and phone numbers. This is for security reasons. Make an exception only when someone gives you his/her business card.

Complete Information on Home for Sale Sheet. Fill in all the blanks thoroughly and clearly. Buyers never get too much information. Spell out words. Use only common abbreviations like "St." for street and the marks ' and " for feet and inches. Other abbreviations aren't always clear and can be confusing.

Call the utility company office if you don't have accurate figures for last year's bills. Call your county tax office if you need exact figures for property taxes.

Your accuracy and care in giving information speaks to the buyers for the care you have given your home.

> **Q.** What about more information? There's a historic story about our home. Would people be interested in that?
>
> **A.** Yes. Any stories about your home would add "color" to the information you are providing. Write it up and include it on a separate sheet.

It would be well worth your time to list specific repairs and maintenance, such as:

> 1983—Outside painted with Fullerton Paint by Joe the Painter, 463-7878.
>
> 1985—Master bath fixtures replaced by Remodeling Experts, 870-4340.

They say that one picture is worth a thousand words. If you are selling your home in the fall when the trees are losing their leaves, show a picture that's different—perhaps one taken in the spring when the azaleas were in bloom.

How buyers rate you for openness, honesty, and dependability in your information giving gets transferred from the paper to the home. It makes sense. If someone provides neat, careful, factual lines of communication, it's not likely that their plumbing and electrical lines are a mess.

Make copies of your completed Information on Home for Sale Sheet. You'll want plenty. This information plus the home itself is the one-two power punch that will help complete the sale of your home.

Have at least 200 copies made. A copy specialty shop will make 200 copies for about $10.

Provide an Offer Worksheet. Prepare to make available copies of the Offer Worksheet. Not having this form right out on your coffee table or kitchen counter when you start to show your home is like starting a car without gas. (Step 6 will tell you all about this worksheet idea, how it came about, and how it can be useful in negotiating an offer.)

> **Q.** I see that many homes take a long time to sell. A home down the street has been for sale for almost a year. Shouldn't we start advertising right away while we're getting forms and papers ready?
>
> **A.** No. Be ready and knowledgeable about getting an offer before the first buyer enters. If you flub handling the first buyer you may be sorry. (See page 56 about respecting that first offer.)

VISITOR SIGN-IN SHEET

Name *Address* *Phone*

___

___

___

___

___

___

___

___

___

___

___

___

___

___

(Reader may reproduce this page.)

Step 2

INFORMATION ON HOME FOR SALE

Address _____

Owners _____ Phone _____

Asking Price $_____ *We encourage all offers in writing and for your convenience an Offer Worksheet is provided.*

Open House Schedule _____

Financing Options:
Assumable Mortgage ( )   Seller Mortage ( )   New Mortgage ( )   Other ( )

Mortgage Lender to Contact: (Name) _____

Address _____ Phone _____

Expenses for the Year 19____:
Property Taxes $ _____   Insurance $ _____   Natural Gas $ _____
Heating Oil $ _____   Electricity $ _____
Association Fee $ _____

Income from Rent $ _____

    Style of Home _____   Year Built _____
    Total Square Feet _____   Roof _____   Walls _____
    Basement or Cellar _____   Type of Heat _____
    Air conditioning _____   Type of Water Heater _____
    Water Softener _____   Size of Lot _____
    State of Overall Structure _____
    Electrical _____   Heating _____
    Kitchen _____   Baths _____
    Number of Bedrooms _____
    Outdoors _____

    List of Rooms   Measurements   Features and Inclusion
_____
_____
_____
_____
_____

Schools _____
Public Transportation _____
The Best Things About This Home _____

(Reader may reproduce this page.)

The Information on Home for Sale (on page 24) can be used most effectively by first enlarging the page to an 8-1/2 × 11 inch size. Then, simply fill in your information and make copies.

OFFER WORKSHEET

This worksheet is for primary discussion while the home is being sold. Only when a legally binding escrow or sales contract is signed by buyers and sellers and earnest money deposited in a trust account will the home be taken off the market.

PRICE OFFERED $ _____

TO BE FINANCED AS FOLLOWS _____

_____

CLOSING DATE _____

NAME _____

PHONE NUMBER _____

(Reader may reproduce this page.)

STEP 3

CREATING YOUR MINI MARKET AT THE OPEN HOUSE

Independent discount buying is moving into every market—designer jeans, air travel, groceries, investments, and insurance. Independent discount buying has built vast chains of clerkless stores like Target and K mart. The success of these stores is evident in parking lots as big as Iowa—all full of cars.

The independent, cost-minded buyers who arrive in those cars will be right at home at your open house. In Step 3 you'll realize how to:

- REAP THE OPEN HOUSE BENEFITS
- OVERCOME THE NEGATIVE, ACCENTUATE THE POSITIVE
- AIM FOR PEOPLE, PEOPLE, PEOPLE
- WEAR NOT EMOTIONS ON THY SLEEVE
- ALLOW TIME FOR YOUR HOME TO SPEAK ON ITS OWN BEHALF

Plan to make your home available to the public frequently. That means setting time aside each week—selling hours, so to speak—when buyers can get inside your home.

When a buyer calls for information, say, "Come on Saturday between one and four o'clock. We'll have the home open and you can look around for yourself." Try to funnel all buyers through the open house. Think of it as your sales arena.

Scheduling a private showing, as real estate agents do, can dampen the spirit of the independent buyers. I wonder how many buyers miss seeing a home for sale because they say, "Oh, never mind" to a private showing.

Recognize, therefore, that it isn't just scouting a bargain that will lure buyers to your open houses; it's also a chance to buy in a manner in which they are accustomed.

REAP THE OPEN HOUSE BENEFITS

Open houses benefit today's buyers by making it easy to buy and providing a relaxed, unhurried environment; independent buyers are used to doing things this way. Open houses benefit you as a seller, too, in the following ways:

- By increasing the number of people who take away favorable impressions of your home, you can increase your profit-potential marketing team. Just as word-of-mouth sells a good book, the word also sells a good home.

- By planning only two or three times a week when you have to turn your home public, you can present your home at its best: floors and furniture dusted and shined; rooms well lighted; window blinds and draperies wide

open; fresh flowers on the table; coffee or tea ready; and a fire in the fireplace.
- By blocking out the time for the open house, you give your full attention to the buyers instead of interrupting your private life.
- By scheduling a time for the open house that is most convenient to buyers you most want to attract, you can increase your odds of a sale. If you live near an area where people work, schedule an open house for after-work hours—for example, Thursday evenings, 4:30 to 7 p.m. The end of the workday is a great time to see a home. I once sold a home to a man who would only look after work. "Because," he said, "when I come home from work that's when I enjoy my home most. I will choose it knowing how it looks at that time of day."
- By scheduling your open house times during a variety of hours, you can show your home to more buyers. Do you live near a church or synagogue? If you do, don't wait to hold your open house at a time after the congregation has passed by and gone home. Time your open house for when services end and people are spilling out past your place.
- By having an established open house schedule, you can easily suggest that casual lookers come to the next one and, thus, broaden your promoting team. For instance, if you meet an acquaintance in the grocery store, you might say, "We're selling our home ourselves."

The acquaintance says, "We have friends looking for a place. They need four bedrooms. How many do you have?"

"Four. We use one as a den, but it could be a bedroom. Drop by with your friends at one of our open houses. We have one every Saturday and Sunday from noon to four o'clock. I hope we'll see you this weekend."

> **Q.** Aren't buyers reluctant to come into a seller's open house for fear of being entrapped by over-eager sellers?
>
> **A.** You can overcome that negative reputation by making the open house a positive, relaxed experience.

OVERCOME THE NEGATIVE, ACCENTUATE THE POSITIVE

To overcome negatives and make your open house a positive, relaxed experience for buyers, and for you as a seller, you should do several things. Prepare the home for unsupervised lookers. Face it: Even with family and friends stationed around the home, every visitor can't be watched every minute. Therefore, the home has to be plucked clean of valuables, breakables, and anything that can be picked up, concealed, and carried out. Also, don't pressure buyers. The word is that sellers come on strong at times to wary buyers. Buyers know they can get in the home, but fear that getting out may be a struggle. Therefore, it's up to you, the sellers, to create a relaxed, nonthreatening atmosphere.

> **Q.** What if you know something is wrong with your house—like the roof needs redoing. Should you tell a buyer that?
>
> **A.** Yes. Say, "If we had stayed, we would be redoing the roof next year. Our price is marked down because we know that buyers will have that expense." You can even say that you've had one estimate and it'll cost about X dollars. "Our price is $90,000, so we'll mark it down X dollars for a new

roof." It's better that buyers hear this from you than learn about it as a surprise later. It gives a comfortable feeling to take in the bad with the good—the devil you know is less scary than the devil you don't know. Don't forget these magic words, "Mark down."

- Be prepared to sell your home by mentioning one or two very big benefits of your home. Especially if you hear a negative comment like, "The yard's too small." Respond with something big and positive: "We have a million-dollar view" or "We will carry a mortgage better than any bank" or "They just don't build homes like this anymore."
- Squeeze the *big* benefits of your home into the conversation with every buyer.
- Dispel buyers' defenses by openness—your willingness to let buyers take in the full measure of your home. Thereby, you will allow buyers to make a thoughtful examination for themselves.
- *Show* your home. Don't push it. Allow the home to sell itself. (I go into more detail about this on page 35.)
- Be enthusiastic about living in your home. Give information openly. When someone shows curiosity about something, explain what's necessary—simply and clearly. Be a wealth of information that's easily drawn out, but don't dominate. Instead, ask questions and listen.
- Tell everyone you are moving. People will be curious. If they don't ask, they will wonder. A simple statement will suffice: "We need a bigger place" or "We want something smaller."

AIM FOR PEOPLE, PEOPLE, PEOPLE

Picture a successful market. A stock market. A supermarket. A farmers' market. What do you see? People. Would it be much fun to go to a summer morning farmers' market and find no one was there? Just the tomatoes? Of course not. Buying is infectious. People catch it from people. So put first things first. First, load your house with people. Later, buyers will separate themselves out from the pack of people. What you want to overhear is something like, "That couple is interested, so this home must be good. We'd better buy it before they do" or "Let's telephone the Cohans to come over—this home seems like just what they've been looking for."

Set the stage for success. Dramatize the open house. Celebrate the arrival of strangers, friends, and relatives. Plan to delight them. Hang a sign on the front door that says "Welcome" and greet people with a smile and a handshake if that's your way. Set a dish of cookies on the kitchen table. Waiting cookies say "Welcome" too.

If someone accepts your invitation to sit down while you answer his or her questions about the home, offer a cold drink or coffee or tea. People walking around generally refuse liquid refreshments.

Alcohol? Never. One seller served wine and ended the open house with a crowd of people. No one left—they telephoned friends to come over. And no one made an offer to buy the home.

Extend the welcome mat. Welcome everyone sincerely. Judging buyers by appearance is doomed to fail. For example, say that you welcomed into your home two men both dressed in jeans and T-shirts. Guessing that one man is the rich bank president and the other man is the poor graduate student, your chances of being right are 50/50 either way.

Most people can't resist the chance to peek inside a home. Expect it and capitalize on it. Warmly greet friends, neighbors, strangers, people coming in from the rain, busybodies, and window shoppers. Some will be buyers, some will tell their friends who are buyers, and some will be there just to look. And in looking, they become the catalyst of the marketplace—people.

As people leave and ask, "Would you mind if I come back with my uncle? my girlfriend? my friend who's a carpenter?" Give them the same answer, "Of course, we wouldn't mind. We'd love to have them."

Sign in all visitors. If your home is in a secure condo building or area, then you have established procedures for signing in visitors. If not, present the sign-in sheet on page 23 and ask each person, "Sign in here, please." Insist on it. People today are used to signing into secure buildings. So, for anyone who hesitates, say, "We'd like a record of who comes through the home." Don't make exceptions.

Q. Is there a way to double check that people are who they say they are?

A. Yes. You could ask everyone for their driver's license or the license number of their car. It's your home, remember; you're in charge. Ask whatever you need to know in order to be comfortable. If you wish, refuse to admit buyers who can't identify themselves.

Besides security purposes, there are other reasons for signing in guests. Getting feedback on what is drawing people is one reason. Ask, "How did you hear about our home?" And then, keep up whatever is working. Stop doing whatever seems to be a waste. Try something else.

Hand out forms. Make sure everyone walks through your home with your information and mortgage literature in hand. These papers are your salesperson quietly saying, "Here's what we're selling. Here's how you buy it."

> **Q.** What if someone says, "Would you take $85,000?"
>
> **A.** Ask them to complete an Offer Worksheet and hand them the form. Point out where the information sheet states: "We encourage all offers in writing." Say, "We need to know what type of financing you are considering; the how and the when of what you'd like to do. We'll consider anything in writing."

People may be curious about the Offer Worksheet. (See Step 6 for more information.) Hand them one and explain that you are using the forms as a way to encourage offers—to get a feel for what buyers are thinking. If they carry off the Offer Worksheet, great—hopefully they'll use it.

Follow up on buyers' interests. Observe your open house visitors to see what interests them most. Stay with them, of course, unless too many people come at one time.

Spend time explaining things and answering questions about whatever is most important to them. Buyers are all different. Some poke into all closets, some are kitchen people and that's where they'll head and plant themselves; some can't resist deep stairways into the basement or cellar. So bend your informational comments in the direction of individual buyers' interests; to different buyers you may highlight your three walk-in closets, or mention that the tile in the kitchen was hand-made in Mexico or point out that the pipes in the basement are all insulated.

WEAR NOT EMOTIONS ON THY SLEEVE

There are scores of helpful books at the library on selling in business. But in selling your home there's a wild card—*your emotions*. Like it or not, in order to sell your home, strangers are going to come into your bedroom and look into your closets. How will you feel about that?

Your emotions can change your owner advantage into a disadvantage. I've seen executives skilled in business diplomacy turn to guerilla tactics while selling their home and repulse buyers.

It's understandable to be emotionally involved with your home, your nest. Plus, you have a big chunk of your money at stake. You have too much at risk to take a chance on hurting buyers—because a hurt boomerangs and ends up hurting you instead.

If your emotions are acting up, quit. Either move out your emotions mentally or list your home with a real estate agent. (See Appendix "Choosing a Real Estate Agent.")

ALLOW TIME FOR YOUR HOME TO SPEAK ON ITS OWN BEHALF

I don't talk much when I show a home. For that reason, a woman client once canceled her listing with me. Since I wasn't talking, she assumed I wasn't selling her home.

I bring this up as evidence of two opposing viewpoints. Is it best to talk or not to talk? Whichever way is natural for you is probably the best way. But, whichever way you go, allow time for the home to talk directly to the buyers.

Once a couple wanted only a two-story colonial home. But they walked into an open single-story modern home—the house spoke, the magic happened—and they bought it. Another time a woman who said she would only buy a home in perfect condition walked into a home needing tons of repairs and made an offer that very same day.

Give buyers space and enough quiet time for "it" to happen. Trust it to happen. A home clever enough to have spoken to you will speak to its next owner. Homes differ; buyers differ. Still, in every sale one thing is the same—the home speaks to the buyers.

STEP 4

REACHING PEOPLE

Think of focusing your promotional activities on a single purpose: To reach people and entice them to attend an open house. Selling the home takes place after buyers see what they like. But first, as they say, you have to get them in the store. To do this you'll:

- MAKE SURE YOUR NEIGHBORS ARE THE FIRST TO KNOW
- POUND A "FOR SALE" SIGN IN YOUR FRONT YARD
- WRITE SIMPLE ADS
- REFUSE AGENTS' ONE-BUYER LISTINGS—AT FIRST
- EXPAND YOUR WORD-OF-MOUTH TEAM

Word-of-mouth news travels fast. Your success in selling your home is directly related to your success in showing your home to people who spread the word.

MAKE SURE YOUR NEIGHBORS ARE THE FIRST TO KNOW

People like to buy houses where they know someone. There are 22 homes on the street where I live. Of the last four sold, only one was sold to a total outsider. The other three were sold either to someone who lives on the street or friends of someone who lives on the street.

The sales went like this: One home was sold to the people who owned the house next door and wanted a larger home; one was sold to the parents of the people across the street and down a few doors; one was sold to good friends of people also already living on the street.

Is this mere coincidence? An isolated happening? No, it happens often. Insider selling of homes is a fertile market. Nurture your supportive team of assistant sellers starting with those closest to you.

Unquestionably, it's not easy to do this at first. Broadcasting to friends and neighbors that you're selling your home yourself is a bit awkward, but you can't afford to neglect this market—especially when you consider that the insider market is the one most likely to produce a sale. So let's try to do something that will make it easy.

Distribute Information on Home For Sale forms. If you recoil at talking to friends and neighbors about the unmentionable—selling your home—consider the following:

- Admit that neighbors are curious. Aren't you when a home in your neighborhood is for sale? I certainly am; I know that my neighbors also are curious. Frequently, I'm asked, "Can

you find out what they're asking for that home?"
- Being curious, wouldn't neighbors appreciate getting the straight facts instead of hearing bits and pieces that bounce around in the telling and retelling of your story?
- Waiting until they find out anyway does you no good. They'll find out, through the back door or over the back fence or, if it's a condo, in the laundry room. Are you taking the most direct route to your most productive market? Heavens no. Have them find out from you and get the facts right.
- For the above reasons, before your For Sale sign goes up, get your Information on Home for Sale Sheet into the hands of your neighbors. Drop it near their mail boxes, slip it under their doors, take a few hours and walk around with it. *Talk* about selling. If you do these things, you'll glean ideas that could be helpful and you'll enlist some neighbors on your home-selling team that could be very helpful.

Or stick a note on the information form like this:

> Help us kick off selling our home.
> Come to a brunch before the first open house
> Saturday, April 11th at 11 a.m.
> Bring a friend if you like—just
> call me with a head count.
> Trish 555-9090

Serve finger food at your brunch: fruit, pastries, or rolled up slices of stuffed meats. The idea is to serve walk-around food that can be eaten while folks look around.

You don't have to be friendly with your neighbors to invite them. You don't even have to know them. Treat your open house preview like the grand opening of a grocery store. Invite "occupants." Expect few no-shows.

Also, when you open up to neighbors, expect them to be on your team. Neighbors *want* your home to sell well. It's in their interest to keep up the neighborhood.

Remember, if you start selling your home by keeping it a secret from your neighbors, you'll surprise them, sure enough. But your surprise may backfire. It may hurt your success. You've slighted people you most want to befriend.

POUND A "FOR SALE" SIGN IN YOUR FRONT YARD

I know, you hate it. But let's face it. There in your front yard, or strung up on your balcony, stands your most effective form of advertising—a sign. It's understandable that you dread putting it up—most people do. However, that bare-faced For Sale sign is unmistakably direct. It gets its forthright message across loud and clear.

> **Q.** Should we spend money on a sign when we only have a limited budget for advertising?
>
> **A.** Yes. The sign is your most important promotion. If you have to, use all of your budget for the sign. Keep back only $10 or so to make copies of your Information on Home For Sale Sheet.
>
> **Q.** Why is a sign so important? Only our neighbors see it.
>
> **A.** This isn't so. Prospective buyers will see your sign. Buyers decide on the neighborhood or area they want first. Then every

chance they get—coming home from work or after going out to dinner—they'll cruise the neighborhood in a "let's see if there's anything new for sale" mood. They become experts on the area. They are likely to make the first offer. (See page 56 about respecting the offer of these expert buyers.)

You'll simply handicap yourself if you try to sell without a sign. I assume, of course, that your area allows signs. If they don't allow For Sale signs, what about a sign outside just when you have an open house? It could just state "Open House" with an arrow pointing toward your place. Most rules allow that option at least.

Q. Where can we get a sign?

A. The Yellow Pages in your telephone book have a helpful section under "Signs." They can be ready-made or made-to-order. Plan your sign carefully. It's your public declaration of your intent to sell. I've seen homemade signs I admire; I've also seen some that look like leftovers from the children's lemonade stand. Someone said that by the look of their sign, you can judge how strong a commitment the sellers have to selling their home by themselves. I take that to mean that if your sign gives up after a week of bad weather, you'll be ready to do the same. Invest in a clear, professional first impression.

If you can set a schedule for open houses that you are sure you can stick to, the sign could read something like this:

For Sale By Owners
Open House
Saturdays & Sundays, 1–4
555–5721

Or, have two signs made: One that just says "For Sale," and another to be put up when you are planning an open house. Such as:

For Sale
By Owners
555–5721

Open House
Next Saturday & Sunday
1–4
555–5721

Display the open house sign in advance whenever you can. Putting the sign up during the week gives people notice so they can plan ahead. A sign sending out its message over several days reaches more people.

A suggestion: At the sign shop, especially one that caters to real estate people, look for helpful ready-made signs. I have in mind the arrows on a stick that say, "Open House." At open house time, place the arrows pointing toward your place on street corners and traffic intersections in your area. Then, be sure you take them down after the open house is over.

WRITE SIMPLE ADS

Classified ads don't always draw people. Before you spend a lot of money, stop the ads if you're getting no response. The important elements you need to state in an ad are that your home is for sale by the owner, the time of your open houses, the price, and the address. Extolling the virtues of the home is unnecessary. Just announce the open house. A prospective buyer has the most important information—the location and the price. Now it's up to the chemistry between the home and the buyer. If the chemistry occurs, other things can be made to work.

Here's an ad to get you started under the "Homes for Sale" classification. Make it single-spaced, all capital letters, and centered.

<pre>
          BY OWNERS $85,000
      OPEN SATURDAY & SUNDAY 1–4
           1789 BOHNS PT. RD.
               555-5721
</pre>

Post an index card on bulletin boards. The card could read:

<pre>
     Home For Sale By Owners $85,000
       Open House Saturday & Sunday 1–4
             1645 Ala Wai Boulevard
              Jan & Sonny Williams
                   555-5721
</pre>

- The card can carry the same message as the classified ad, but with a little more information. Add your name. It doesn't cost you any more money and you are likely to reach someone who knows you or whose friend is a friend of yours.
- A card mailed to the personnel office of a big company will generally be posted. Attach a note such as, "Please post this on your employees' bulletin board. Thanks."

Q. Where can we find bulletin boards?

A. You'll find them in work places, shopping centers, laundries, schools, information centers of condos, health clubs, and office buildings. Bulletin boards are often social centers for announcements of the latest events. I know one condo building where no resident would think of walking into the building without first checking the bulletin board.

REFUSE AGENTS' ONE-BUYER LISTINGS— AT FIRST

As you begin reaching people, expect calls from real estate agents.

You can respond to these calls with, "We choose to sell our home ourselves, thank you." Most agents will respect that. However, expect agents who specialize in your area to ask to see your home. They want to keep abreast of homes for sale in "their" area. They will also harbor a hope that you will end up listing your home with them.

An agent may say, "I have buyers who may be interested in your home. Would you sign a one-buyer listing contract so I could show them your home?" If that one buyer buys your home, the fee for this contract may be the full 6 or 7 percent commission rate or it may be less.

I suggest that you say to the agent, "Not now. We're in the midst of aggressively promoting our home ourselves. Call me in three months. If our home hasn't sold, we'll consider listing with you then."

Q. Why shouldn't we go ahead and sign the contract? We don't want to miss out on any buyers.

A. I don't think you'll miss those buyers. Buyers decide first on the area they want, then they look for a home. If you are located in their desired area and have your sign out, they'll find you.

I previously told owners to agree to these one-buyer listing contracts. Then I watched the muddle that our neighbors got into when they tried to sell their home themselves while giving one-buyer listings to agents.

I decided they didn't have the best of two worlds, they had the worst. 1) They lost the benefits of their own promotional momentum. They had to remove their For Sale By Owner sign to accommodate agent showings. 2) They had no benefits of agent promotions through the multiple listing catalog. Yet, if they sold through an agent, they would have to pay the full commission.

NOTE: If you cannot aggressively promote your home, list it with an agent who can. (See Appendix "Choosing a Real Estate Agent.")

EXPAND YOUR WORD-OF-MOUTH TEAM

Besides neighbors, who else can you deputize as assistant sellers? Who will be interested in reading your Information on Home For Sale Sheet?

What about your family, cousins, in-laws, the people at work, in the car pool, at the golf course or bridge club, the Bible study group, the bowling league, the health club, or the exercise class?

Even if you feel pushy saying to someone in these groups, "Would you like to see information on the home we're selling?" I suggest you give it a try. Do your own market testing. See what response you get.

Don't underestimate the form—it is a powerhouse of information. People are as curious about your home as they are about the celebrity homes in *Architectural Digest.* If for no other reason, most people would like to see your asking price. Make the information work for you. Sharing your information brings more people onto your team and working for you.

Mail information. To people who telephone in response to your advertising with questions about the property, say, "We have an information sheet about the house. Would you like me to send you a copy?"

- If they want information take their names and addresses. Have envelopes and stamps ready. Drop it in the mail that same day. Keep their phone numbers. In a week or so, telephone them to ask if they received the information and if they had any questions.

Keep reaching out to buyers. You are sure to hear "How's it going?" from insiders frequently while your sale is gestating. Give those asking an update. "We're getting lots of people at the open houses, but no offers yet." Or, "We had one offer. We countered it and they didn't come back, but we think we might hear from them again."

- Respect the genuine interest of neighbors and friends. Your sale affects them. They may meet buyers tomorrow and tell them about your home. So don't turn off any asset you have in your favor.
- If you are in the midst of negotiating a price, keep the figures to yourself. Don't disclose the amount until the sale is closed and the title has passed to the buyers. Keep quiet even though you have a contract to sell in hand.

The reason for keeping quiet during negotiations is that any outside influence can muddy the waters. During negotiations it's time to deal solely with the buyers.

NOTE: Record expenses of promoting your home. For income tax purposes, keep a record of your receipts for advertising, signs, printing costs, the cost of this book and forms you use, envelopes, stamps, and refreshments you serve at open houses.

STEP 5

FETCHING A PRICE

There's no better way to describe getting the best price for a home than the auctioneers' term "fetching a price."

Rarely is a home put up on the auction block. Understandably, sellers are reluctant to take the chance that the price they can get in the few minutes of an auctioneer's chant is the best one that's available.

However, the graphic phrase "fetching it" adapts well to getting the best price. Using the term keeps a reminder before you that the price of a home is *not* cast in cement. Therefore, in Step 5 you'll find out how to:

- ASK A "GOOD" PRICE
- KNOW WHAT YOU CAN BUY FOR THE MONEY
- WEIGH YOUR ASKING PRICE AGAINST FINANCING
- LISTEN TO BUYERS
- FREE YOURSELF FROM MYTHS
- HONOR THY FIRST OFFER

Abandon "shoulds." Believing that there is a price a home "should" sell for is the single most common obstacle to selling a home.

Your home is like anything else for sale. Price will be determined by a coming together of what buyers are willing to pay and you are willing to accept.

ASK A "GOOD" PRICE

What's a good asking price? Simply put, it's lower than comparable homes for sale.

> Q. Won't buyers make offers when they think the price is too high?
>
> A. Not usually. I think it's because the too high price sours them on the home itself. But with a good price, aggressively promoted, you have better possibilities of getting your asking price. Hopefully, with more than one interested buyer competing, you'll get more than your asking price.
>
> Q. Will checking out comparable homes for sale give us an idea of a good asking price?
>
> A. Yes. That will give you an idea of how your buyers compare your home. You'll be amazed at the scatter pattern of asking prices. I've seen $10,000 to $20,000 differences asked for almost the same home.

Accept real estate agents' offers of a free market evaluation. Usually, even when you explain that you plan to sell your home yourself, agents will come out and give a free evaluation. That's the way they get listings. They hope, if you decide to list, you'll call on them.

Ask the agents for a computer printout of the addresses and prices of homes sold in your area. Knowing the sold price of homes gives you insight into how serious buyers are looking at price. The closer you target your price to buyers' sights on price, the closer you'll hit a sale.

Q. Where else can we find out about the sold price of homes?

A. Call your county recorder. If the recorder doesn't have that information, he or she will know who does.

Q. Should we tell buyers that our price is lower because we don't have to pay a real estate commission fee?

A. Yes, by all means tell them. That's today's sellers' anthem, "We will not be undersold." Buyers follow that tune like the Pied Piper.

Q. If we don't get to keep the real estate commission fee, why should we do the work selling our home ourselves?

A. You definitely end up not paying a fee. What's flexible is the price at which you end up selling your home. In a market with few buyers you—because you're not paying a commission—can mark down your price to entice a buyer to buy. In a market with many buyers, you can sell at a higher price. Either way—many buyers/high price or few buyers/low price—you keep the commission fee.

Step 5

Use the markdown technique. If you're giving a reduction in the asking price for a new roof or for new carpeting, show $88,000 as the asking price less a $3,000 markdown for new carpeting.

> **Q.** But what if we have to have a certain price in order to sell at all? Say we must have $20,000 cash from this home. Otherwise we won't move; we'll stay.
>
> **A.** Then, of course, don't sell unless you get your price. Just because you encourage offers, it doesn't mean you have to accept an offer that's too low. Set any bottom price you want, but if you have to have $20,000 and you get five offers over five months that only get you $7,000 in cash, you might consider taking your home off the market for now.

Never, never drop the word "asking" and say the price is $85,000. That shuts the door on all but the most feisty of buyers. Saying "asking price" leaves the door ajar. Buyers can slip in offers, make a bid, and feel they are not out of line in doing so. The idea is that if you are open to offers, hopefully you'll get more than one buyer bidding up the price and get more than your asking price.

Ask a price as high as will still make your home look terrific. Meanwhile, hold the thought as stated on the Information on Home For Sale Sheet: "We invite offers and will respond to all offers within 24 hours."

KNOW WHAT YOU CAN BUY FOR THE MONEY

I sold a town house for $90,000 that had an asking price of $120,000. Apologetically, I said to the seller, "You must feel awful to have sold it so low."

"On the contrary," the man grinned, "We're breaking out the champagne. We got a better deal on the place we're buying than these guys are getting on the place we sold."

I tell you this because most home sellers buy another place when they sell a home. What you can buy with the money you take for your home makes a difference. Economists call it the *real* value of money.

To answer wisely the question, "How much (or how little) will you take for your home?" you have to know the answer to the question, "What can I buy for the money?"

Thus these words to the wise—shop for what you will buy before you sell. (See page 9).

WEIGH YOUR ASKING PRICE AGAINST FINANCING

If you're thinking about price, factor in the manner in which the buyer pays for the money—the financing. The only time you can consider price without factoring in financing is if you're talking about cash. Yes, $85,000 cash from one buyer is exactly the same as $85,000 cash from another buyer. However, if buyers have to pay interest on the $85,000, what they pay in interest makes a difference. If a buyer has to pay 13 percent interest on an $85,000 mortgage he or she will pay $11,050 extra the first year. If interest is 11 percent, the first year's cost will be only $9,350.

> **Q.** Do we have to worry about financing *before* we have an offer and even *before* we have a buyer?
>
> **A.** Definitely. You can't detach price from financing. They're two sides of the same coin. The price you can get depends on the financing the buyer can get.

Q. But financing is the buyer's problem. Why should we concern ourselves as sellers?

A. You should be concerned because your selling price depends on it. If interest rates are high, it means your price will have to be less. Conversely, if interest rates are low, you can expect a higher price.

If the sellers of the town house above had to pay a much higher interest rate on the place they bought, compared to the rate on the place they sold, they might not have such a good deal. The higher interest might have eaten into the lower price.

Price alone doesn't tell the whole story. I go into more on balancing financing and the price in Negotiating an Offer on page 59.

LISTEN TO BUYERS

The idea of encouraging offers is to go fishing for the best offer you can get. In the process, you learn what buyers are fishing for. Say frankly to buyers who ask about price, "We are serious about selling and we will look seriously at all offers."

Openness to low offers, even expecting them, doesn't mean you have to settle on one. Maybe you will, maybe you won't. Ideally, by encouraging all offers, you'll encourage buyers to compete with each other. They'll bid up the price. Maybe you'll get more than you're asking.

Think of price as a harmony with the home and with the buyers. In order to strike a deal, it takes the balance of ready-and-willing buyers and ready-and-willing sellers in harmony at the same time. It's when sellers insist on playing solo that they have trouble. One couple I know wouldn't look at any offers. "Don't bring us an offer," they would say. "It's our home, we'll dictate the price." And there, with their minds made up, they sat on their property—and sat, and sat.

FREE YOURSELF FROM MYTHS

Take a careful look at widely accepted myths so they don't get in the way of successfully selling your property. There are three major myths about the price of a home:

> *Myth 1:* There is a fixed "market value" for property that can be predicted with certainty.
>
> *Truth:* Belief in "market value" is comforting, but stupid. The Market Value Myth is the opiate of home sellers. It's to blame for most For Sale signs rusting, tilting, and aging in front yards. Sellers often have strong convictions of the market value of their homes.

Clearly, the prices for which other similar properties have sold can give you a clue as to the price for which your home might sell. But a price for a home is not preordained, nor is it fixed. Remember how price is tied to financing? There's just one of the many factors that undercut the Market Value Myth. Weather, population growth, construction industry trends, and a host of other variables also bear individually on the price of each home for sale.

For these reasons, each home must create its own mini market. What happens with other home sales is unlikely to be duplicated exactly—ever.

> **Q.** Can't we expect our place to sell for what a similar home sold for down the street?
>
> **A.** No. It could be the same or more or less. Each seller, buyer, home, and selling situation is different. Your deal is unique, one of

a kind. Looking at it that way makes it possible for you to get the best price sooner.

The best selling price comes from getting the most people to see your home and encouraging offers, regardless of its so-called market value.

Myth 2: Salesmanship and sizzle will sell your home and get you your best price.

Truth: Not today. Salesmanship—in the sense of hype and pressure tactics—will send buyers sneaking out the back door.

Think about it. When was the last time a salesperson "sold" you anything you hadn't sold yourself on first? If anything "sold" you, I bet it wasn't someone. Whether you bought a car, a toaster, or olive oil, I bet what sold you was product knowledge and your own evaluation. You were probably "sold" by answers to questions like, "What will I get?" or "What will I give for it?"

Myth 3: Relocating buyers—those who are coming to your area to work for a big company and are unfamiliar with local prices—will pay a high price for your place.

Truth: It's time to bury this myth. It's been dead for years. Sure, maybe a Martian will drop down with a sales contract in hand, but not an Earth dweller. Relocators have learned their lesson and they are smart. Why else would companies write big checks to transplant them and their families?

HONOR THY FIRST OFFER

The following is not a fairy tale; it is true. It's repeated as often as the rhymes from Mother Goose. Sellers learn this lesson the hard way.

Let's say the sellers receive an offer after the first open house. The offer is low, and the sellers are impressed with themselves.

"See," they say, "how quickly someone wants to grab our home?" They are slightly disappointed with the low offer. They say, "We'll get our price with no sweat. We won't even respond to these guys. Trying to pull a fast one on us, are they? We'll show them."

Their asking price is $100,000. The offer they reject (by ignoring it) was for $85,000.

The story continues: Now it's six months later. The sellers are still waiting for an offer better than the $85,000. Then, expectations eroded by time, optimism deflated, the sellers accept a lower price yet—$80,000.

Write this lesson in red neon flashing lights and hang it on the wall: Honor thy first offer. The best buyers you will reach are cruising the neighborhood. They have been doing this for a while and are ready and able to buy. They are just waiting for the appearance of new For Sale signs.

Why are these buyers best? They are best because:

- These buyers aren't just looking, they've been house shopping for some time. They aren't watching the market, they're driving the market up or down by making offers.

- These buyers, as a rule, have made low offers before. They know how to do it and they know the prices for which other properties have sold. It's no wonder they know a good buy when they see one. They've earned a honorary home-buying Ph.D. on homes selling in your neighborhood.

- Such buyers may negotiate their offer or they may continue to wait and cruise. If after careful thought you cannot accept their offer, make a counter offer (explained on page 73). Never simply reject it, and never just ignore it by failing to reply.

NOTE #1: Don't fall into the trap of self-torture. Selling to the buyer who makes the first offer can plant bitter second thoughts: "We sold too easily. We sold too low." That is not necessarily so. If you hadn't sold, you might have ended up like the sellers in the classic story—waiting and waiting then selling for less.

NOTE #2: Don't stay too long in the market. Generally, homes for sale over six months don't finally fetch a better price, they fetch a worse one. Rheumatoid suspicion sets in after a while. Buyers suspect something is wrong with the home. They think, "We would love to make an offer on that place. But we'd better not. It could be that we'd get stuck with whatever is wrong with it."

Q. How long should we take to sell our home?

A. You should take no longer than six months to sell your home. Take your home off the market if after six months you are still holding out for your price. Store the For Sale sign in the garage. Leave it there until one of the following happens:

1. Homes around you start selling at prices you would accept.
2. You decide to be flexible and go not for *your* price but the *best* price you can get.

STEP 6

NEGOTIATING AN OFFER

Trumpets sound; the main event is about to begin. On the table before you is *an offer*. It's not what you hoped for. It *never* is.

Look on the positive side. You now have a buyer. You're two-thirds of the way to a sale. You have 1) yourself, the seller and 2) the buyer. Now all you need is 3) the agreement.

In order to keep that buyer interested and be able to come to an agreement, in Step 6 you'll find out how to:

- TOUGHEN UP FOR SHOCKINGLY LOW OFFERS
- LIMIT NEGOTIATIONS TO THE INFORMATION ON THE OFFER WORKSHEET
- REFUSE TO LOWER THE PRICE FOR AN OFFER WITH CONTINGENCIES
- CONTACT YOUR TEAMMATE—THE MORTGAGE LOAN OFFICER
- WEIGH, AGAIN, FINANCING WITH PRICE
- USE TIME TO YOUR ADVANTAGE

Step 6

There's a gorgeous turn-of-the-century mansion in my town that is used as executive offices for a business. Recently one business sold it to another. I was on the sidelines of this event; I watched and was impressed. To work out the deal, the principals—the buyers and sellers—sat down and came to an agreement on the most important item of the sale. The next day the buyers wrote the sellers something like this: "This letter is to put in writing the terms of our verbal agreement yesterday. As per our agreement, we will pay $300,000 for your building. The price will be subject to us getting a 10 percent loan from the First National Bank before the closing date of November 1, 1989. We will have our attorney write a legally binding sales contract and will be in touch with you."

I latched onto the idea with an Offer Worksheet. The procedure goes like this:

- Negotiate the price, financing, and closing date following the Offer Worksheet (see page 26).
- When these vital items are settled you, the sellers, should have your lawyer or escrow or title agent write a full legal sales contract. The buyers, having already agreed to the important items, will check over the sales contract with their attorney. If there is no impediment, all parties sign.

Q. How is an offer usually made by a real estate agent?

A. Usually the agent for the buyer fills in the blanks on a form called a Legal Sales Contract or Purchase Agreement. The form, having been written by a lawyer, becomes legally binding once all the blanks are filled in and signed by the buyer and seller. The form is sold in some office supply stores.

The full sales contract with an earnest money check is presented by the buyer's agent to the seller's agent and the seller. The full sales contract is then negotiated.

> **Q.** Why don't you suggest we buy a sales contract form and go the route of a real estate agent?
>
> **A.** I don't suggest this for several reasons. First, without legal guidance, signing a legal document can get you into trouble even when a real estate agent is involved. Second, the price, financing, and closing date are not legal matters. Buyers and sellers negotiate this the best when it's done directly. And finally, paying a legal fee before a legal document is needed is a waste of money.

TOUGHEN UP FOR SHOCKINGLY LOW OFFERS

Sellers frequently feel insulted if someone makes a very low offer. Relax, though, and don't take it personally. Brace yourself to expect shockingly low offers. When you encourage all offers, you'll get the high and the very low. Value even the low ones. Say to the person who made the offer, "Thank you. We've considered it. It's too low, but we'll make a counter offer."

> **Q.** Why do you say to value such an unacceptable offer?
>
> **A.** There are several reasons: You have a serious buyer in hand; you've hit your target, so score one point for you. Remind yourself that that low price may be a feeler, a place to start negotiations. And even if the negoti-

ations go nowhere, you've heard feedback from a buyer. You know something you didn't know before. Maybe you don't like what you hear, but you now have something to think about. Finally, if you get several offers you think are "unacceptable" it may be time to rethink your price or terms. What else could you settle for?

The home selling game is played by sellers wanting to get the highest price and buyers wanting to pay the lowest price. These goals are as well defined as the goals on the opposite ends of a football field. The more you're ready for low offers, the more you know how you will respond, and the better prepared you'll be for the encounter.

Q. Won't buyers expect to discount the 6 or 7 percent real estate commission fee off our price?

A. Some may expect this. Remember, the price you end up with will be determined by the overall number of buyers out there and how many you have reached. Whether you give a discount for the fee or for any other reason depends on how many other buyers want your home.

LIMIT NEGOTIATIONS TO THE INFORMATION ON THE OFFER WORKSHEET

Negotiate only the price, financing, and closing date. These are the most important items to agree upon. Everything else, including the small print of a full legal contract, can wait. If you can agree on price and financing, waiting a few days for a full legal sales contract is a fair trade-off. It lets you concentrate on first things first.

Q. Why should we use the Offer Worksheet?

A. When you use it, there is no confusion as to the figures you are discussing. You'll have no need to ask, "Are we talking about $85,000 or $87,000?" Also, price, financing, and closing date are presented as a package. The "how much," "how," and "when" are clearly related for you to evaluate.

The document itself is a helpful form with which to work. You can keep it overnight, sleep on the pros and cons, and start up again the next day where you left off. And when you finally *do* agree to a deal, you can take the written offer intact to your legal expert in order to have a written sales contract drawn up.

Sell the property as stated on the Information on Home For Sale. If buyers want to include your dining room table and eight chairs in the price, and you haven't included it on the information sheet, what do you do? Try to include the personal property most buyers expect and resist pressure to add more. Include your washer, dryer, and refrigerator. If buyers can't be discouraged from adding more, state on the information sheet: "We will include the dining room table and eight chairs now in the dining room *if* an offer is accepted from the undersigned buyer(s)."

> **Q.** Why do you say to discourage the buyers from including additional personal property?
>
> **A.** I discourage it because you can start negotiating that and it sidetracks the more important consideration—the price of your home.

Get any inclusion of personal property in writing before you get into the world of price. The Information on Home For Sale Sheet and the Offer Worksheet should cover all the items of your agreement—the *what* you are selling for *how much*, *how*, and *when*.

REFUSE TO LOWER THE PRICE FOR AN OFFER WITH CONTINGENCIES

There are two kinds of "ifs" you may face in an offer. When a buyer makes an offer of $85,000, with a new mortgage at 10 percent interest, the financing is a contingency. It's a necessary one. It means buyers will pay this specific price *if* they can get that specific financing. Since they can't get a firm mortgage commitment without a signed sales contract, there is no way to get around it. So you have to expect it and accept financing contingencies.

The contingencies that I say to refuse are the *ifs* such as: *if* you fix the roof or *if* my mother likes it or *if* the buyers sell their present home. Refuse to lower your price when the buyer's offer is followed by any *if* —other than one tied to financing.

> **Q.** Why do you say not to lower our price with an *if* tied in?
>
> **A.** Because it's not a square deal. Buyers and sellers are not negotiating equally—the sellers commit to a price and the buyers have a

loophole. So seal up the loopholes, get rid of the *ifs*, and, thus, firm up exactly what is being sold. Then get down to the business of price.

Ask the buyers directly, "How do you want to handle removal of this contingency so we can get down to discussing price?"

If the contingency is for you to fix the roof, you have three choices: You can fix the roof, you can insist the home be bought "as is," or your can negotiate the cost of a new roof and agree to mark down any price you agree to by this amount.

If the contingency is for a mother's approval, have them bring mother by. If she likes it, remove the contingency and negotiate. If she doesn't, give back the offer.

If the contingency is for buyers to sell their home, return the offer. Ask them to come back when their home is sold. If they offer to remove the contingency of first selling their home be leery. Thoroughly look into how they will manage to buy your place at the scheduled time if their own home hasn't sold yet. Can they demonstrate how they'd handle two payments at once?

Q. Why do you say not to accept an offer that is subject to buyers selling their place first?

A. Because it leaves you in limbo. You stop selling your home and wait for them to sell their home, but you have no control over that sale. It could be a ghastly home; overpriced or badly promoted.

Q. What if we agree that we can go on trying to sell our home and if we get an offer before their home sells, then they agree to withdraw their original offer?

A. That would be fine. Just be sure you have that written in legal terms.

CONTACT YOUR TEAMMATE— THE MORTGAGE LOAN OFFICER

Here is where the loan officer—whose literature you've been distributing—comes onto the scene.

Ask the potential buyers to telephone the mortgage loan officer. The loan officer will know the information needed to qualify the prospective buyers for a new mortgage. From a telephone call the loan officer can find out if the buyers' financial status is close enough to qualify for you to negotiate the price.

A formal credit check is in order after you have a sales contract. (See Step 7.) Then, whoever lends the money for a mortgage will check the buyers' credit.

Also, your home will be appraised by the mortgage lender after you have a sales contract. Your home, as well as the buyers' credit, must qualify for the mortgage amount.

WEIGH, AGAIN, FINANCING WITH PRICE

Q. Why do we hear that the price we get will be the lowest if we cash out?

A. It's simply time applied to the value of money. Money you get today is worth more than money you expect to get down the road. Therefore, if you carry any kind of financing for the buyers, you can expect to get a higher price.

Here is a rundown on the affect of financing on price. Generally, the lowest prices are for cash or for a new mortgage which gives cash to sellers. The highest price is for a sale in which the sellers hold the mortgage and act as bankers for the buyers.

With cash or a new mortgage, you can expect the lowest price for these reasons:

- Cash buyers are the most rare.
- Buyers who can take out a new mortgage are less rare; but it takes a sound, solid financial record to qualify, and it is costly. Further, the buyer will consider the cost of the new mortgage as a part of the price of the home. Say a new mortgage costs $4,000 in points, origination fees, and other added costs. If the buyer is willing to pay $85,000 for your home, but has to pay $4,000 of that for a new mortgage, you can expect to get $81,000.

Q. What if we, the sellers, pay that $4,000 cost for a mortgage?

A. You still get to keep only $81,000, even though the buyer pays you the $85,000. You might tell yourself the price was $85,000, but if you pay the $4,000 mortgage cost, you only wind up with $81,000. (Keep these costs in mind when you compare "sold" prices of other properties. Try to find out who paid the new mortgage costs.)

With an assumable mortgage, you can expect a little higher price for the following reasons:

- More buyers qualify.
- Buyers pay lower up-front costs to assume an old mortgage than to create a new one.
- Both buyers and sellers look upon a good, large assumable mortgage that compares favorably with a current new mortgage as an added value

of the property. If your home could sell for $85,000 with a new mortgage, you may expect to get $86,000 or $87,000 with a good, large assumable one.

With an assumable mortgage where the sellers carry a second mortgage, you can expect the next higher price for these reasons:

- There are more buyers.
- This kind of financing is attractive for the same reasons as the assumable mortgage, plus there's the added attraction that the down payment required can be flexible. Sellers accommodate the buyers by taking a note for part of the cash payment.
- On the $85,000 home expect $88,000.

When the sellers carry a first mortgage, you can expect the highest price for these reasons:

- The greatest number of buyers can buy. The only restriction is whatever the sellers agree to.
- The up-front cost is the lowest because there are no points or origination fees.
- The terms and down payment can be anything that the buyers and sellers agree to and for which the law allows.
- On the $85,000 home expect to get $89,000.

To sum up the effect of financing on price, expect at least a 10 percent spread between a new financing or cash deal, and a deal where you carry the financing. The scale goes like this on a $85,000 home:

$81,000 for new financing or cash
$86,000 for an assumable mortgage
$88,000 for an assumable plus a seller note
$89,000 for seller financing

Q. Does the type of financing we require of buyers make a difference in our ability to sell the place?

A. Yes, especially if you are in a tight market and sales are slow. Take a good look at the financing you expect. Ask your loan officer to suggest financing where you can expect the most buyers. If you must cash out, make sure you encourage all offers, even very low ones.

When home sales are slow, property that is easiest to finance is easiest to sell. Salability varies along the same pattern as the above financing varies. That means, if you want cash, fewer buyers can qualify and your property is the *least* salable. Moving to the opposite extreme, if you are able to carry a seller mortgage, the greatest number of buyers can qualify, and your property is the *most* salable.

Ask yourself, "What does this price, at this time, mean to me?" Opinions and advice on pricing will come from everyone when you sell your home. In one deal I handled a while ago, I discovered that the man who lived next door to the home I was trying to sell would telephone the seller immediately after every prospective buyer toured the home. He always said, "Don't take less than $120,000." He was looking out for himself, not the best interest of the seller. I met the man one day and he told me, "I'll do everything I can to keep her from accepting a lower price." He didn't add, "Even if it means my neighbor, who desperately needs to sell, doesn't sell." So my advice is to listen to all the advice-givers, then make up your own mind. Do what's best for you.

The Seller's Price Worksheet, on the following page, filled in appropriately will give you a basic overview of how you would come out if you accept a given offer.

USE TIME TO YOUR ADVANTAGE

Time is a helpful ally to sellers in negotiations. Time plays a variety of roles such as:

- "Can you take a minute? We each know what we want. Let's sit down together and talk it over. We can settle the price now or identify where we have differences."

- "Give us time to think it over. We have to get used to this price. We'll call you tomorrow. Meanwhile, we'll give it some thought."

- "Let's take time to get a sense of what the buyers are thinking. Is this offer a feeler? Will they go higher?"

- "What would selling at this time mean to us? What offers do we see coming in the future? What have we had in the past? Today, realistically, is this offer the best we see? What's it worth to sell now and have the sale behind us tomorrow?"

SELLERS' PRICE WORKSHEET

Buyer's Name _____

Price Offered _____

Less Expenses:

Mortgage Owed $_____

Other Notes Owed _____

Liens _____

Taxes Owed _____

Legal Costs _____

Financing Costs _____

Advertising Costs _____

Escrow Costs _____

Settlement Costs _____

Other Costs _____

Total Expenses $ _____

Price Received by Sellers $ _____

(Reader may reproduce this page.)

Step 6

> **Q.** With an offer in front of us, how can we evaluate it?
>
> **A.** Try writing lists. Call one list "What's good," the other "What's bad." Then rate each item according to its importance on a scale of 1 to 10. Getting all your cash quickly may be a 10 if you're buying another home immediately and need cash to buy the other place. All cash may only be a 5 if you're buying a place that is smaller and requires only a small amount of cash as down payment.

Keep in mind that there is no right or wrong way to rate each item. A familiar saying in the stock market applies here: "Sometimes *bulls* make money, sometimes *bears* make money, but never *hogs*."

Trust your instincts, but back them with a clear-headed evaluation of each offer's merits.

> **Q.** What if we get two offers at the same time?
>
> **A.** Tell each buyer that you have another offer and you will be considering them both together. Allow the buyers time to change their offer if they wish before a specific deadline. Then look at them both and counter or accept only one. If you make a counter offer, make it clear that it is good for only 24 hours. If that buyer rejects the counter, make a counter offer to the other buyer. But, don't get two counter offers out there at the same time. Both may accept—and you have only one home to sell.

Respond always. Resist the temptation to reject any offer. If you only accept the closing date, at least counter the offer by changing everything else. But get that offer, however it is weakened, back into the buyers' hands.

Why must you respond? Because you won't sell if you don't have an actively interested buyer—and you can't read buyers' minds. Leave the door open for each potential buyer to become the new owner.

Q. Should we continue having open houses while considering an offer?

A. Emphatically, YES! You want to keep the buyers worried that someone else may buy it.

Counter the offer. If you are comfortable negotiating around the kitchen table with the buyers, then by all means do it that way. Make changes together like the executives did when buying and selling the mansion used for offices. Make a pot of tea or coffee, exchange ideas, keep cool. And remember, if you can't accept the offer as presented, counter it.

Q. What if the buyer leaves the offer and, after we think about it a while, we want to make some changes. How do we change the price with a counter offer?

A. Say the buyers offer $75,000 and that is not enough for you, simply cross out that price and write in $80,000. Adjust the mortgage another $5,000. Call the buyers and tell them you have a counter offer.

Q. Can buyers counter our counter offer?

A. Sure. Let's say the buyers receive your counter offer. It's still too high for them, but they still would like to own your place. Here's what they do:

1. Cross out your $80,000.
2. Write in $77,000.
3. Send it back to you.

When the form gets messy from counters to counter offers, buyers or sellers can start a clean offer form from where they left off. The point is to keep offers and counter offers going back and forth working toward a deal both the buyers and sellers can accept.

Accept it when it's right for you. If and when the offer is acceptable to all buyers and sellers, be certain about the following items:

- You agree to the price, financing, and closing date written on the offer.

- The property is exactly as it was presented on the Information on Home For Sale Sheet.

STEP 7

CLOSING THE DEAL

You have two giant hurdles yet to clear: 1) A signed, legally binding sales or escrow contract with an earnest money check. 2) A legally binding closing or settlement of the sale. In Step 7, to help you carry the deal over the hurdles, you'll:

- ANTICIPATE THAT YOU'LL BE NEEDED
- CONTACT YOUR TEAMMATE—THE LEGAL EXPERT
- KEEP ON TOP OF THE SALE
- STICK—LIKE GLUE—TO THE CLOSING DATE
- CONGRATULATE YOURSELF

It's not over yet. In charge now is your lawyer, escrow agent, or title company. Even so, there's a good chance it won't be over unless you "mother" the deal all the way to the closing table. Help, give support, and, therefore, make finalizing the sale easy for the buyer.

Every sale toddles like a two-year-old child—unsteady on his or her feet, falling up and down. Will your sale close? Whoops! You almost lost that buyer!

An entire book could be written with lists of reasons why signed deals fell through. But a close examination would show the same reason at the heart of each failure: No one was helping it along.

> **Q.** If the buyer wants to arrange for the sales or escrow contract to be written, who arranges the closing?
>
> **A.** The seller arranges the closing. But, if there is any delay in the written sales or escrow contract, expect to arrange to have it written yourself. You, as the seller, have to keep on top of the execution of the sales contract, depositing the earnest money with your legal expert, and the arrangements for the closing.

ANTICIPATE THAT YOU'LL BE NEEDED

You're packing to move. You have a million things to do. But the most important detail is to accommodate the buyers. Until the closing, expect a steady stream of calls such as:

- Buyers call with a question—Is the roof charcoal gray or black?
- Buyers call again—Can they come over with a decorator to measure the windows for curtains?

- Buyers call once more—Uncle Horace is in town; could they bring him over to see the home they bought?
- Lawyer calls—Where is the divorce decree?
- Lender calls—When can they schedule a time to do the appraisal?

You should simply expect to be inconvenienced even after you've signed a sales or escrow contract. The reason is that the sales contract only says the buyer will buy and you will sell. You still need to make sure the buyer does buy and you do sell. It's up to you if the deal gets closed and you get your money.

Some buyers take responsibility for holding the sale together. But you shouldn't take the chance that they will, only to later find out that they didn't take the responsibility. See that it's not too hard for them. Buyers have to arrange financing. They could run into obstacles, run out of steam, get discouraged, or lose interest. It's in *your* best interest to be positive, upbeat, and expect that all obstacles will be overcome. If there is a document on the other side of town that one lawyer needs and there is fussing about whose job it is to pick it up, you should plan to drop everything and go get it.

Sure you're buying another place yourself. You have plenty of demands on that side, too. But just ask yourself, "What if we don't have time to oversee this sale?" You can't buy the other place until this one sells. So make sure you put first things first. Close on this deal, get your money from the sale, and then carry on with your purchase.

CONTACT YOUR TEAMMATE— THE LEGAL EXPERT

Re-enter the legal expert, lawyer, or escrow or title agent whom you contacted in Step 2. Have a legally binding sales contract written according to the terms you and the buyers have agreed to in the offer.

When the sales contract is signed by the buyers and the sellers, have an earnest money check from the buyers deposited with your legal expert.

> **Q.** How much should we expect in earnest money?
>
> **A.** At least $1,000 for each $100,000 of the selling price is what you should expect.
>
> **Q.** Why so much?
>
> **A.** You want to be sure the buyers are serious because you will be taking your home off the market.
>
> **Q.** Will the earnest money be used as a down payment?
>
> **A.** Yes. So it's not costing the buyers anything extra to put the money into a trust account at this point.
>
> **Q.** What happens to the money if the sale falls through?
>
> **A.** It depends on the reason for the failed sale. If the buyers can't get financing, the earnest money is returned to the buyers. For this reason, you should have the buyers telephone your chosen mortgage loan officer immediately. If the buyers are not going to be approved for a mortgage, get back to selling your home as soon as possible.

If the sale falls through for any reason other than nonapproval of financing, you need the input of your legal expert as to whether or not you are entitled to any of the earnest money.

Q. Is the Offer Worksheet legally binding?

A. No. It's not a document; there are no signatures. The Offer Worksheet is a tool for agreeing on terms so that a legally binding sales contract can be written.

Q. What preparations do we need for signing the sales contract?

A. What you need should all be ready if you've been following the steps in this book. You should:

1. Be ready to accept the price, financing, and closing date which you have agreed to with the buyers.
2. Be ready to contact all parties who are listed as owners of the property for signatures.
3. Be ready to submit your proof of clear title to whomever your buyers designate to examine the title. Your legal expert should have earlier advised you on removing any impediments to a sale. (See Step 2.)

KEEP ON TOP OF THE SALE

Someone in the office of your legal expert will be assigned the task of closing your sale.

Stay in contact with whomever is in charge of the closing. Also, keep within easy reach the telephone numbers of the buyers, their attorney, the lender, the escrow agent, the title company agent, and the closer. Don't give up your authority over the sale—no matter how complicated the proceedings may become.

Ask the closer to inform the buyers, as soon as possible, of the exact amount of money that they will need at the closing and whether a personal check will suffice or a certified check is required. Don't feel that you are bothering the closer or the mortgage lender by making these demands. You're paying for the closing. And, in home selling, it's the squeaky wheel that gets the deal closed.

Cut down on lawyer's costs. If you use a lawyer, you can do a lot to keep the costs down.

> **Q.** What will a lawyer charge?
>
> **A.** Lawyer's rates vary; it depends on what you need. Ask what they'll charge you. Don't engage a lawyer's service without knowing the cost. You might want to ask how you can keep costs to a minimum. Then keep in mind that a lawyer's time is money, and that a lawyer's value to you is in looking out for your legal protection. See that the time your lawyer spends on your account is for legal matters. If you need hand holding, call a friend.

Here are a few ways to cut legal costs:

- Telephone your lawyer with questions only when a note won't do.
- Search out documents yourself. Go get them or have them sent directly to whomever needs

them—the lender, lawyer, or title/escrow company.
- When closing the sale, use the same lawyer that you had in preparing and updating documents for your home.
- Keep in mind that the lawyer's clock is ticking at an expensive hourly rate. Use all the time you need. But use time efficiently on legal problems.

NOTE: Ask that both you and the buyers receive copies of all documents three days before settlement. Insist on it. In three days you and the buyers can thoroughly read the document, ask questions, and clear up any problems.

STICK—LIKE GLUE—TO THE CLOSING DATE

Missing the closing date doesn't negate the sale. The closing date is a target date. At least that's the legal opinion generally held.

However, don't think of it as changeable. Push for that date. Keeping the closing date as an inflexible goal keeps everyone on target. Be firm with the lender, the lawyers, the buyers. Be braced to keep saying, "No, we can't delay the closing, sorry."

Expect that obstacles will appear daily. Most will seem insurmountable. But, to anyone who says it can't be done, say, "Nonsense." Ask, "What is needed to do the job?"

The fact that any home ever gets sold is a minor miracle—the miracle of someone refusing to let anything get in the way. In the end, the closing date may have to be rescheduled. But only postpone the date when it becomes utterly impossible for some party to the transaction, usually the lender, to be ready. If the

Step 7

money won't be there you have a good reason to set another date.

If the money is ready, head for the closing table, even if there are some problems to resolve. Things can sometimes be resolved best when two parties sit across a table and face each other one on one.

Just remember to keep on top of everything. And keep the money you save by selling your home yourself.

CONGRATULATE YOURSELF!

APPENDIX

CHOOSING A REAL ESTATE AGENT

You may be faced with listing your home with a real estate agent. Nationally, 75 percent of homes are sold this way. You can't ignore the possibility.

How do you choose the best agent? Here are some dos and dont's:

DO look for names of agents on "For Sale" signs in your neighborhood. The companies they work for matter little. Companies are all alike. It's the agents who are different. It's the agent who sells your home. Or lets it sit.

DO call each agent for an interview and ask questions. What is he or she presently selling? How are they going about it? What have they sold? How would they propose reaching buyers for your home?

DO remember "success breeds success" is an important rule, but not the only one. One seller told me she chose a new agent whose only listing was a home across the street. The seller met the agent and admired her commitment to the task of selling. The seller listed her home, knowing it was only the agent's second listing. Voila! It became her first sale.

DO explain to friends in real estate that you are choosing an agent who specializes in homes like yours. Agents are licensed by the state to sell real estate within the state. But to expect an agent selling downtown condominiums to be the best agent for your suburban ranch-style home, and vice versa, is illogical.

DO set the asking price yourself. Expect the agent to assist you with (1) a list of homes sold in your area in the last six months and their sold price (2) a list of homes for sale in your area and their asking price, and (3) the price suggested for your home by a gathering of agents called together at your home by your agent.

DO negotiate the commission before you sign a contract. It's the law! Each commission for each home is negotiable. Insist on it.

DO know what services you will receive for the commission you'll be expected to pay. Get it in writing. Don't accept the basic: "Your home will be listed in the Multiple Listing Catalog and other agents will help find a buyer." What will *your* agent do to find a buyer?

DO have in writing your expectattions, such as:

- The "For Sale" sign in your front yard will state the agent's phone number and the open house days and hours.

- The agent will arrange financing with a local lender.
- The agent will prepare a sales brochure with a picture and information about your home.
- The agent will report to you at least once a week. Together you will judge the sale's progress. What's working? What isn't? How best to continue?

DO keep control. A good agent will earn his of her commission. However, you, the owner, are the one at risk to lose a great deal of your money. Relentlessly ask questions. Why? Why not?

What should you watch out for?

DON'T be intimidated by what you don't know. Nobody knows everything.

DON'T tie yourself to a long-term listing contract. Begin with three months. Then evaluate the agent's performance. If it's good, list again. If not, change agent's.

DON'T choose an agent because he or she suggests asking a pie-in-the-sky price. This can be costly for you. Agents have been known to suggest a too-high price to nudge sellers into signing a listing contract. Then, when the home sits a few months, losing its new-arrival bloom, the agent suggests lowering the price.

DON'T sign any contract that signs away your precious right to your day in court. Some agents have begun asking sellers to sign an agreement stating any differences that may arise be settled by arbitration.

DON'T call the local Board of Realtors if you have a disagreement with an agent. The Board is a private trade association whose members are people in the real estate business. The Board supports their members' interests.

If your disagreement is over more money than a small claims court allows, see an attorney or contact the consumer advocate in the office of your local or state attorney general. Explain your problem. Ask for guidance.

INDEX AND GLOSSARY

Abstract of Title: A chronicled history of all recorded documents affecting ownership of a property—such as title holders, loans, liens, and death and marriage certificates.

Adjustable Rate: The interest charged on a mortgage that fluctuates, up or down, depending on the current interest rate paid on government-secured loans of like term.

Advertising: see Classified Ads.

Agent: A person licensed by the state to engage in the business of helping to bring buyers and sellers together and negotiate prices. An agent must work for a licensed broker, 44–45, 60, 61; Accepting offers of a free market evaluation, 50

Amortization Schedule: A table showing the amounts of principal and interest due at regular intervals, and the unpaid balance of the loan after each payment is made.

Appraisal: An estimate or opinion of the value of property.

Assumable Mortgage: A former owner's obligation which new owners can take over and continue the prescribed payments, 66–67.

Balloon Payment: An amount due, in a lump sum, on the principal of a mortgage at a specified date—either during or at the end of the mortgage term.

Biweekly: Payment terms in a mortgage to reduce the amount of interest due. Payments are made every two weeks instead of every month.

Board of Realtors: A trade association for those who sell homes. It is *not* a government body; the Board of Realtors is an association of private companies. A member is called a Realtor.

Broker: A person licensed to act independently who engages—like an agent—in the business of helping to bring buyers and sellers together and negotiate prices. A broker can form his or her own company, become a partner in a real estate company, or work independently.

Bulletin Boards: 43–44.

Buydown: Money advanced by an individual (buyer, seller, or builder) to reduce the interest rate on a mortgage.

Buyers' Broker: Currently, this role is without guidelines and is open to national debate. The only *true* buyers' broker, who is 100 percent on the buyers' side, is the person with whom the buyers have signed a contract—the person acting for, and being paid by, the buyers. Payment can be whatever the broker and buyers have agreed upon. Payment, however, should not be a split of the sellers' broker's fee.

Cancellation Document: A written statement that voids a written sales contract. It must be dated and signed by all parties who signed the original sales contract.

Certificate of Title: A written document stating that the title to a piece of property is legally vested in the present owner.

Classified Ads: 42. Not copying real estate companies, 19.

Closing or Settlement of Title or Escrow: The finalizing of the sale, including delivery of a deed, financial adjustments, the signing of; notes, and the necessary disbursement of funds, 76–82; date, 81.

Closing Costs: Money required to be paid by buyers or sellers of a property being sold by one owner to the next. Included can be mortgage loan origination fee, discount points, title insurance, credit report, property appraisal, survey, attorneys' fees, and fees for preparing documents.

Comparables: Property used in appraisals to determine like value, 10; planning your sale promotion by studying your competition, 18–19; comparable homes for sale, 50.

Contingencies: 64–65.

Contract for Deed/Land Contract: A method by which sellers, in order to allow buyers the time to pay for the property, keep the deed until the amount stated in the contract is paid in full.

Conventional Mortgage: A mortgage loan not insured by the Federal Housing Administration (FHA) or guaranteed by the Veterans Administration (VA).

Counter Offer: 73–74.

Credit Report: A verification of borrower's ability to repay a loan.

Deed: A document that moves the title (ownership) from one party to another. It is not the title, but it is one evidence of title.

Down Payment: The amount of cash that buyers pay toward the price of a property. Included is earnest money paid at the signing of the sales contract. Not included is money paid for points or other up-front fees charged by the lender for issuing the mortgage.

Due on Sale: A requirement in the small print of some mortgage contracts stating that if the property is sold, the loan must be paid in full. Therefore, the mortgage is not assumable.

Duplex: A single building with two separate housing units.

Earnest Money: A monetary deposit held by a third party—a lawyer or escrow or title agent—giving evidence of a buyer's good faith when signing a sales contract, 16, 61, 75, 78.

Easement: The right of one party to use the land of another party for a specific purpose—to enable sewer or other utilities to be laid or to allow for access to a property.

Emotions: 35.

Equity: The value of property, less what is owed on it. This is usually referred to as the owner's value.

Equity Home Loan: A second mortgage available when the value of a home exceeds the first mortgage.

Escrow: A situation where an impartial person or company holds documents, money, and instructions for a sales transaction for the buyers and the sellers.

Fair Market Value: The price paid for a property by a knowledgeable and ready buyer to a knowledgeable and ready seller.

Fee Simple: The greatest possible interest a person can have in land ownership.

FHA Mortgage: A mortgage loan made by a private lender to a private borrower that is insured by the Federal Housing Administration (FHA). Since the FHA insures the loan, it sets standards for the condition of the home and the financial condition of the borrower. Many first-time home owners use FHA mortgages because of the low down-payment requirement.

Financing: Weighing price against, 53, 66–70.

First Mortgage: The claim at the head of the line to take possession of the property over other claims should the borrowers default.

Fixed Rate: The interest charged on a mortgage that stays the same for the life of the mortgage.

Foreclosure: A procedure in which property pledged as security for a loan is sold to pay the borrower's debt.

Information on Home For Sale, 20–21, 24, 25, 38, 45–46, 52, 63, 74.

Interest: The money paid for money. This is usually stated as an annual percentage of the principal owed.

Joint Tenancy: Ownership of a property by more than one person; each owns equal shares and has equal right of possession. (Different from Tenants in Common.) When one owner dies, those shares pass immediately and equally to the surviving owner or owners.

Land Contract/Contract for Deed: A method by which sellers allow buyers time to pay for the property. Sellers, in essence, finance the purchase. Buyers take possession of the home. Sellers keep the deed until the amount stated in the contract is paid in full.

Lawyer or Legal Adviser, 12, 16–18; have telephone number, 18; contact, 77–79; cut down on costs, 80, 81.

Legal Description: A manner of identifying a property in government records.

Lien: A claim or hold of one person on the property of another person to secure payment of a debt or obligation. The intent is that the property cannot be sold or the owner receive money until the debt is paid.

Listing Agent/Sellers' Agent: The person who contracts with the owners to sell the property, and if successful, collect a fee.

Listing Agreement: An employment contract between a property owner and a broker that gives the broker the right to offer the property for sale and collect a commission when it sells. One buyer, 44–45.

Loans: see Mortgages.

Lock In: A method used, after an application for a mortgage has been approved, to have the lender set aside in reserve the actual dollars at a specific interest rate and with fixed up-front costs. Each lender will have a policy as to how long before the scheduled closing date the buyer must "set" (lock in) the interest rate and points.

Mark Down, 5, 52.

Market Evaluation: free, 50.

Marketable Title: A title that for all practical purposes is clear and one that a prudent buyer of real estate would accept.

Monthly Payments: An amount set in the mortgage agreement covering the interest owed for the previous month and part of the principal.

Mortgage: A loan that applies to real estate. Borrowers sign a promissory note to repay the loan and give the lender the right to take possession of the property if the borrower defaults on the loan. 13–16, 66–69.

Mortgage Loan Officer: Choose to qualify buyers, 11–13; have telephone number, 16; contact, 66.

Mortgage Qualifying: 11, 12, 13.

Multiple-Listing Service: A local network of cooperating real estate companies that share their business and split their fees. Usually these companies operate under the umbrella of the local Board of Realtors.

National Association of Realtors®: The dominant real estate industry trade association in the United States.

Negotiating the Offer: 59–74.

Neighbors: Make sure they're the first to know, 38, 39, 40.

Offer: Negotiating, 59–74; honor thy first, 56–58; toughen up for shockingly low, 61; counter, 73–74.

Offer Worksheet: 20, 21, 22; form, 26, 34, 60, 62–63, 79.

Open House: 27–36; benefits, 28, 29, 30.

Origination Fee: A charge by lenders to prepare loan documents.

Personal Property: The possessions in a home that are easily moved and not intended to stay with the home unless specifically mentioned in the sales contract.

P.I.T.I.: The cost often included in a monthly mortgage payment. It stands for principal, interest, taxes (property taxes), and insurance.

Points: A cost of interest payable in advance of obtaining a mortgage loan. The payment of points lowers the loan's interest rate. Points sometimes change daily.

Possession Date: The day when buyers may move into the property.

Price: The total required to buy a home—cash down payment plus the money borrowed, 49–58; negotiating, 47; free yourself from myths, 55–56; sellers' Price Worksheet, 71.

Principal: The amount of debt, exclusive of accrued interest, remaining on a loan.

Private Mortgage Insurance: A policy written by a private company protecting the mortgage lender against loss from a mortgage default.

Promissory Note: A written promise to pay a specific amount at a specific time.

Property Taxes: The costs levied locally by the city, county, or state. The amount is usually determined by the size and location of the property.

Purchase Agreement or Sales Contract: A legal document between buyers and sellers stating their intentions and conditions to finalize a sale.

Purchase-Money Mortgage: A mortgage held by sellers.

Quitclaim Deed: A document giving up all interest, title, or claim to a property by a grantor, but not containing any warranty of title.

Qualifying for a Mortgage: 11, 12, 13, 66.

Real Estate Agent: see Agent.

Real Estate Broker: see Broker.

Real Property: The land and everything of a permanent nature built into a home.

Realtor®: A term registered by the National Association of Realtors for use by its members. This membership is usually a prerequisite for membership in the local multiple-listing network.

Sales Contract or Purchase Agreement or Escrow: A legal document between buyers and sellers stating their intentions and conditions to finalize a sale, 60, 61, 75, 77, 79.

Seller Financing: A financial arrangement between buyers and sellers with terms and conditions agreeable to all parties, 16, 67, 68.

Settlement: see Closing.

Sign: 40–42.

Single Agency/Exclusive Agency: A recent development in the real estate market whereby agents commit to being loyal to one party in the transaction—either the buyer or the seller. Exclusive agents do not cooperate with the opposing agents, as in a multiple-listing arrangement, nor do they share business or split fees.

Sub Agent: The agent in a multiple-listing network who is the salesperson to the buyers; he/she works for the seller as an assistant to the sellers' agent. Incorrectly, but commonly, called the buyers' agent.

Tenants in Common: A type of ownership where there is more than one owner on a property, each owning a separate share; interests need not be equal and there is no right of survivorship.

Terms of Mortgage: The conditions under which a mortgage is given—interest rate, duration, and manner of repayment.

Title: The evidence of the right of ownership in property.

Title Insurance: A policy against defects in the title not listed in the title report or abstract.

Title Search: An examination of public records to reveal the state of ownership on a property.

Torrens: A method used by a public authority to register land titles.

Trust Deed: A manner of mortgaging a property involving three parties—the lender, the borrower, and a trustee who holds the promissory note and deed to the property.

VA Mortgage: A loan available to eligible armed service veterans. The loans are long-term and allow for low down payments. The loans are made by private lenders to private, eligible borrowers. The Veterans Administration (VA) protects the lenders against loss.

Visitor Sign-in Sheet: 20; form, 23.

Warranty Deed: A guarantee that good title is being conveyed.